Exploring Caves

PIONEER EDITION

By Glen Phelan

CONTENTS

Into the Light. *A caver climbs from the depths of Lechuguilla, a cave in New Mexico.*

Weird and Wonderful Caves

Caves may seem quiet and peaceful, but they are alive with movement.

------ By Glen Phelan ------

Caves are more than tunnels. They are **habitats,** or places where plants and animals live. Frogs, snakes, and many other animals call caves home.

Water makes most caves. Water slowly wears away rock. It cuts out tunnels and rooms. Water then creates amazing shapes in the cave. For example, water can make rock cones on the floor and ceiling.

Life in a Cave

After a cave forms, animals move in. To learn about them, we will explore Mammoth Cave. It is in Kentucky. It is the largest cave on Earth. About 100 kinds of animals live there.

Cave dwellers are usually called **troglodytes.** They live in many parts of the cave. Some are near the cave opening. Some race around dim tunnels. Others live in the darkest rooms. Each area forms a different habitat.

Timber rattlesnake

Into the Dark

The cave opening is called the **entrance zone.** Lots of animals spend time there on hot days. They like the cave's cool air.

Other animals live deeper in the cave. They are in the **twilight zone.** The twilight zone is beyond the cave's mouth.

Here light is dim. Air is cool. Spiders crawl about. Crayfish swim in ponds. Snails live on the floor and walls.

Beyond the twilight zone lies an even dimmer area—the **dark zone.**

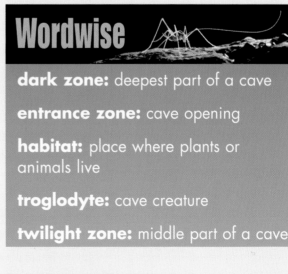

Creepy Crayfish. *Like many cave dwellers, this ghostly white crayfish has no eyes.*

Down in the Ground. *Bats are probably the best known cave critters. This ghost bat lives in Australia.*

Deep and Dark

The dark zone lives up to its name. It is always dark. The air is stale. Most animals could not live here. Some could not live anywhere else.

Many animals in the dark zone are white. Most are also eyeless.

Dirty Water

Deep under the ground, caves may seem far away. Yet what we do on the surface affects them.

Dirty water can seep into a cave. The water can destroy the cave's beautiful rocks. It can kill many troglodytes as well.

It takes millions of years to form a cave. It takes a long time for animals to move in. It takes much less time to destroy a cave habitat.

How might a cave affect life on the surface above it?

Wordwise

dark zone: deepest part of a cave

entrance zone: cave opening

habitat: place where plants or animals live

troglodyte: cave creature

twilight zone: middle part of a cave

SAM ABELL (CAVE); © MARY ANN MCDONALD, CORBIS (BOBCAT); © BRECK P. KENT, ANIMALS ANIMALS (SNAKE); B.G. THOMSON, PHOTO RESEARCHERS, INC. (BAT); © CHIP CLARK (CRAYFISH, CRICKET).

Explore a Cave

Water from a stream cuts through a kind of rock called limestone to form a cave.

A chamber is a large room.

Stalagmites rise from the cave floor. Drops of water leave limestone specks on the ground.

A passage is a tunnel cut through limestone by water.

Moving water is very powerful. It can wear away limestone rock. It can make long tunnels and huge rooms in the limestone. The diagram shows some of the features that water can create.

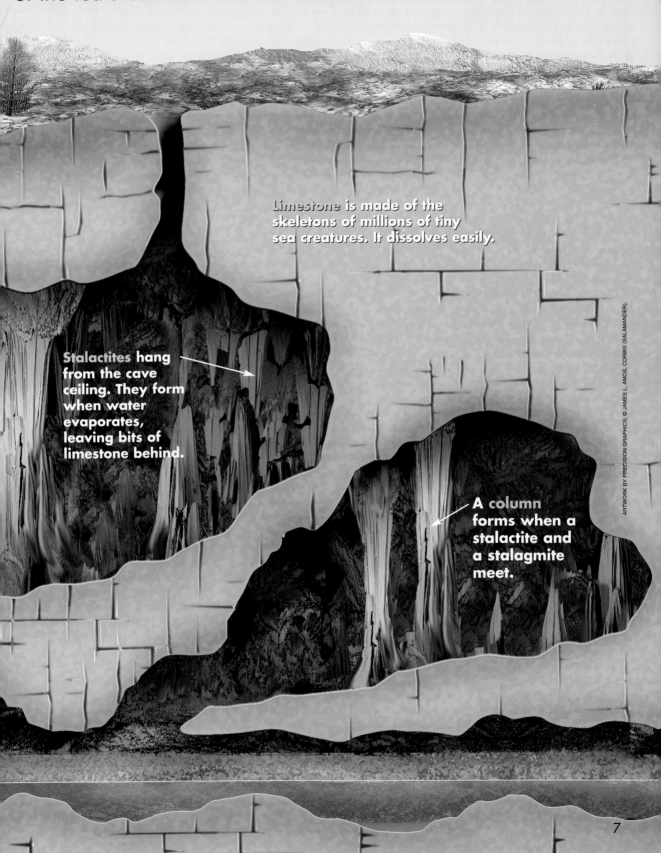

Limestone is made of the skeletons of millions of tiny sea creatures. It dissolves easily.

Stalactites hang from the cave ceiling. They form when water evaporates, leaving bits of limestone behind.

A column forms when a stalactite and a stalagmite meet.

Be a Smart

Going Underground.
The right tools and careful planning help people enjoy the features in a cave.

Caver

Exploring a cave is fun. It can be dangerous too. Here are a few things all cavers need to know.

Choose the right cave.

Some caves are easy to explore. Others take a lot of skill. Choose a cave that matches your skill level.

Be prepared.
Get permission before going into a cave. Then be sure to bring the right tools.

Stay on the trail.
Caves are fragile. One wrong step could harm the cave. So hike only on the trails.

Have fun.
Caves are full of beauty. So make the most of your trip. Plan carefully. Pack well. And enjoy your adventure!

INGRAM PUBLISHING (COMPASS); TIMOTHY LARGE, SHUTTERSTOCK (BOOTS); TIMOTHY ARMES, SHUTTERSTOCK (HELMET); LOGOS, SHUTTERSTOCK (CARABINER); PHOTODISC (ROPE)

Caving Tools

Serious cavers use these tools of the trade to explore a cave.

Compass. *A compass helps cavers find their way through twisting passages.*

Boots. *Cavers need sturdy boots that won't slip on the wet cave floor.*

Helmet. *Cavers wear helmets to protect their heads.*

Carabiner. *A carabiner is a special metal loop that cavers use for safety. It hooks easily onto ropes.*

Rope. *Cavers use ropes to climb steep cave walls.*

A Hidden Cave

Rare Beauty. *Crystal cave features cover a passage deep inside Lechuguilla Cave.*

Caves can be fun places to explore. But some caves are very fragile. Only scientists can go inside. That is true for Lechuguilla Cave.

A Different Kind of Cave

The cave is in New Mexico. It is the deepest cave in the country. It is also the third largest. That is not all that makes the cave special.

Most caves form as water runs down through rock. Lechuguilla did not. It was carved out from below. Water mixed with chemicals. Then it bubbled up and into the rocks.

Hidden Creatures

People first found the cave in 1986. They had to dig an opening. Until then, the tiny animals inside had been closed off from the world.

Scientists think the animals may have been around for millions of years. They might give us clues about Earth's first living things.

Lechuguilla has many hidden treasures. They are changing how we think about life on Earth.

Caves

It is time to take a look at what you have learned about caves.

1 How do most caves form?

2 Why is a cave a habitat?

3 What kinds of animals live in caves?

4 Why should you be careful when you explore a cave?

5 What makes Lechuguilla Cave so special?